IMAGES
*of America*

# THE MILITARY HISTORY OF THE CAPE COD CANAL

Two of the author's daughters, Alanna (left) and Tara Butler, stand on remnants of a Panama Mount at the East Point Military Reservation, located in Nahant, Massachusetts. The photograph was taken in December 2001 when Tara, a senior airman in the U.S. Air Force stationed at Ramstein Air Force Base in Germany, was home for Christmas furlough. Alanna is a junior at Swampscott High School, in Swampscott, Massachusetts. This concrete and circular rail system is identical to gun mounts situated at the Sagamore Hill Military Reservation, which defended the Cape Cod Canal during World War II.

IMAGES
of America

# THE MILITARY
# HISTORY OF THE
# CAPE COD CANAL

Capt. Gerald Butler

ARCADIA

First printed in 2002.

Published by Arcadia Publishing,
an imprint of Tempus Publishing, Inc.
2A Cumberland Street
Charleston, SC 29401

Printed in Great Britain.

Library of Congress Catalog Card Number: 2002100080

For all general information contact Arcadia Publishing at:
Telephone 843-853-2070
Fax 843-853-0044
E-Mail sales@arcadiapublishing.com

For customer service and orders:
Toll-Free 1-888-313-2665

Visit us on the internet at http://www.arcadiapublishing.com

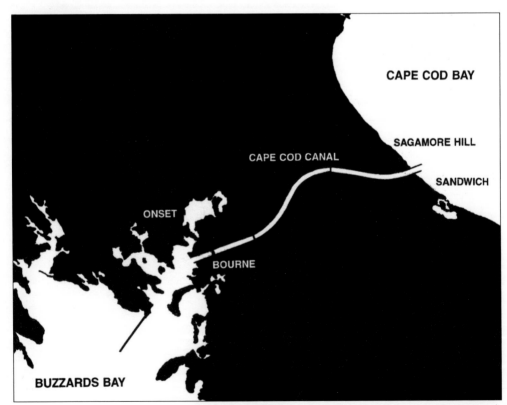

This map shows the locus of the Sagamore Hill Military Reservation, at the easterly approach
to the Cape Cod Canal during World War II, and Buzzards Bay, at the westerly approach.

# CONTENTS

# INTRODUCTION

The primary purpose of the Cape Cod Canal is to provide a safe navigation channel for vessels seeking the shorter and safer route through the isthmus of Cape Cod. The U.S. Army Corps of Engineers operates the Cape Cod Canal and, on average, saves 135 miles of open sea travel around the tip of Cape Cod.

The history of the Cape Cod Canal traces far back to explorations of the region by Miles Standish in 1623. When he observed the narrow neck of land that joins Cape Cod to the mainland, he also noted the valley and two bodies of water that were separated by less than a mile in distance. The thought for a canal was conceived, but it would not be until 1880 that the first attempt to construct a canal was initiated. Nearly 500 laborers armed with shovels and wheelbarrows attempted to carve a canal. Because of meager funding, however, the project was terminated within a short period of time.

The land area, including and surrounding Sagamore Hill, was used at varying intervals for shipbuilding, farming, and an expansive golf course. In 1899, the Boston, Cape Cod and New York Canal Company, under the direction of August Belmont, was granted a charter to construct a 100-foot-wide canal, which commenced on June 19, 1909. The limited-depth canal was opened on July 29, 1914. By May 16, 1916, the contractors attained the full depth of 25 feet.

The route of the original canal did not exactly follow the existing canal but rather wound its way through upper Buzzards Bay and Hog Island. This quickly became a problem that resulted in a number of serious accidents and inconveniences to mariners.

The Federal Railroad Administration took control of the canal during World War I. After negotiations lasting nearly 11 years with the Boston, Cape Cod and New York Canal Company, the canal was purchased by the federal government and opened as a toll-free waterway. During World War I, the *Perth Amboy* incident illuminated the imperative requirement for protection against German submarines lurking offshore. It would be years later that decisive military plans would be developed.

From 1935 through 1940, the canal was modified to its present configuration of 540 feet wide, with a length of 17.4 miles and an approach channel 32 feet deep. Canal construction also afforded two highway bridges and a vertical lift railroad bridge (reportedly the third longest vertical lift drawbridge on the continent) to be constructed over the canal.

Prior to World War II, joint U.S. Army and U.S. Navy strategists proposed to use the canal as a haven for shipping with protection by coastal defense forces and systems from the Harbor Defenses of New Bedford, Massachusetts, and Newport, Rhode Island. On the eastern side of the canal, U.S. Navy contact mine fields were to be established, while the U.S. Army would provide rapid-fire guns and mobile 155mm GPF gun batteries at strategic locations, including Sagamore Hill. The U.S. Coast Guard would assume overall jurisdiction for the canal's operation and security during a wartime footing.

It is at this point that the military history of the Cape Cod Canal begins.

# One

# THE ORIGIN
# OF DEFENSES

Although perplexing, the military history of the Cape Cod Canal began at Fort Ruckman, in Nahant, Massachusetts. In September 1940, certain National Guard units were federalized, including coast artillery and antiaircraft regiments. Accordingly, Battery C, 241st Coast Artillery Regiment (Harbor Defense), was stationed at Fort Ruckman and assigned to Battery Augustus P. Gardner, a massive 12-inch, long-range gun battery.

Battery C performed artillery drills and maintenance upon Battery Gardner from September 1940 through October 1941. At that time, a regular army unit from the 9th Coast Artillery Regiment (Harbor Defense) took station at Fort Ruckman and manned the gun battery, as shown below. Battery C was then transferred to Fort Dawes, Deer Island, in Winthrop.

This is one of the last formations of Battery C, 241st Coast Artillery Regiment (Harbor Defense), at Fort Ruckman in October 1941. Elements of the battery have been divided into platoons, as shown above.

Personnel were originally quartered in squad tents while contractors completed new barracks and structures at Fort Dawes. In this view, soldiers are readied for personal and full-field inspection in front of pup tents.

Prior to construction of temporary buildings at Fort Dawes, the Resthaven Cemetery had to be exhumed and remains transferred to Fort Devens in Ayer, Massachusetts. This 1940 image depicts the joint military and civilian ceremony at Resthaven honoring soldiers from the War of 1812 through the post–Civil War era.

When the new barracks were completed at Fort Dawes, a grand martial ceremony was held, complete with an official flag-raising ceremony that took place involving all of the fort's personnel and officers from the headquarters of the Harbor Defenses of Boston.

Although these two photographs do not show Fort Dawes, they were taken at nearby Fort Heath in Winthrop and accurately depict a typical sandbagged 155mm cannon emplacement under construction by the gun crew.

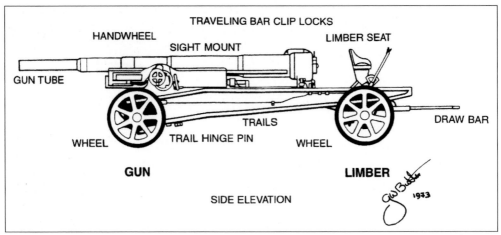

Shown in this diagram are the primary components of a 155mm cannon in its traveling, or towed, position.

This is a view of a 155mm cannon atop the highest hill at Fort Dawes. Limbers for the gun can be seen to the rear of the cannon, and a manhole-style observation station is located directly to the rear right of the gun carriage. The original Harbor Defense Seawards Station and signal mast is situated to the far right of this October 1941 image.

Members of Battery C relax after an arduous artillery drill on a 155mm cannon at Fort Dawes on a warm October day in 1941.

Intensive artillery drills began in mid-November 1941 that included towing the 155mm cannons from their firing position to various locations throughout Fort Dawes. In this image, a powerful tractor is towing a 155mm cannon by means of a wheeled limber arrangement. The limber—shown with seated gunners—was an intermediate assembly that connected the trails

of the gun carriage together to form a central tow point. Due to Deer Island's wind-swept location, a tarpaulin has been draped around the breech and recoil mechanisms of the gun carriage proper. This prevented abrasive sand clogging the delicate elevation and traversing systems and the finely machined surfaces of the weapon's working components.

Because of the advancing war in Europe in November 1941, local harbor defense systems maintained a more militant posture. Guards were posted at the Fort Dawes 155mm gun batteries 24 hours a day, equipped with steel helmets, gas masks, bayonets, ammunition, and loaded rifles, as seen here.

# Two
# DEFENDING THE CANAL

Immediately following the declaration of war in December 1941, elements of Battery C were transferred from Fort Dawes to Sagamore Hill, Cape Cod Canal. A convoy of three large cargo trucks, towing two 155mm cannons and carrying ammunition with two squads of soldiers departed Fort Dawes shortly after the evening meal. A command car, shown here, led the convoy.

This is a photograph of the Sagamore Hill advance detail officer in charge, 2d Lt. William Ostlund, Coast Artillery Corps.

An advance detail of noncommissioned officers is standing next to one of the tactical cargo trucks used to transport the cannons and men to Sagamore Hill.

The advance detail arrived at the forlorn site shortly before 5:00 a.m. the next morning. By 12:00 p.m., the two guns had been set up in "hasty field positions," temporary observation stations were established, and ammunition was ready. This image shows the weary but smiling gun crew just before 12:00 p.m. on that long day.

A relaxed moment follows a formal guard mount at Sagamore Hill in December 1941. Soldiers are fully equipped with field equipment, heavy overcoats, and leggings to keep warm during the long evening sentinel duty.

The little time afforded for relaxation was generally spent near Sagamore Hill due to the severe threat of alerts. In this view, two soldiers from Battery C are inspecting the carcass of a mammal near the entrance to the Cape Cod Canal.

On December 14, 1941, the main contingency of Battery C arrived at the Sagamore Hill Military Reservation and was quartered at the Ella F. Hoxie school nearby. Quarters at the school were for a short duration but extended through spring 1942. The sergeants and corporals bunks were placed on the stage of the gymnasium, and the privates used floor space for their cots.

On February 2, 1942, elements of Battery C were transferred to nearby Camp Edwards and absorbed into a larger unit designated the 50th Coast Artillery Regiment. Later, the 50th Coast Artillery Regiment was transported to Fort Dix in New Jersey, becoming part of the first task force (Task Force 0051N) to depart from the United States for Europe.

During January 1942, two additional 155mm cannons were towed to Race Point (at the tip of Cape Cod) and were set up on the beach about a half mile from the Coast Guard Station. The detail—under the command of 1st Lt. Vahan Vartanian, who was later major general and adjutant general of Massachusetts—consisted of two squads of men quartered and fed at the Race Point Coast Guard Station. This detail lasted for a period of two months under extremely cold and wind-swept conditions, as seen in this photograph of the cannon encrusted with snow and ice.

The first commanding officer of the Sagamore Hill Military Reservation and captain of Battery C, 241st Coast Artillery Regiment (Harbor Defense), was Capt. Whitely Ackroyd, Coast Artillery Corps.

At varying intervals, music was provided at the gun site by talented musicians of Battery C, as seen in this photograph of Private Garrand, a guitarist, resting on the hood of an army cargo truck.

The dire threat of an enemy using various methods of gas warfare was paramount at all military installations in 1942. Technically recognized as chemical warfare, the use of toxic substances harks back to primeval battles when opposing forces used favorable winds and smoke from burning pitch to disrupt opposite forces. During World War I, trench warfare was culminated by the use

of deadly toxins, including blister, chlorine, and mustard gases. Protection against chemical warfare was developed during and after the war, resulting in new gas masks, filters, and protective ointments. In this image, soldiers are wearing the newest gas mask apparatus of the period, walking through a gas training exercise at the Sagamore Hill sand flats in March 1942.

Training for gas warfare consisted of using smoke and tear gas grenades at the Sagamore Hill sand flats. In the photograph above, soldiers march in formation into a smoke-filled area. Notice the gas mask carriers—or containers—on each soldier's left side. Below, the alarm "Gas!" has been issued, and the soldiers have withdrawn gas masks from carriers, put them on, and adjusted them as necessary.

Pvt. Marlin Ball, dressed in a winter full-field uniform, prepares for evening guard mount and inspection at the Sagamore Hill Military Reservation. The steel helmet is attached to the rear of his combat pack, and the gas mask is under his left shoulder.

Prior to new barrack and structure construction, telephone poles and communications were installed. In this March 1942 view, a telephone lineman at Sagamore Hill begins splicing and connecting new communications wires by way of a pole-mounted junction box.

*Three*

# SAGAMORE HILL:
# THE GUN SITE

This is a photograph of an unidentified soldier in prone firing position with a Browning Automatic Rifle (BAR). The newly constructed barrack is to left, and Sagamore Hill is to the right rear *c*. July 1942.

Capt. Whitely Ackroyd, post commander and commanding officer of Battery C, 241st Coast Artillery Regiment (Harbor Defense), is seen here in front of the post headquarters building with company clerk looking on c. July 1942.

Here is a candid snapshot of 1st Sgt. Eugene J. Lavoie in front of the post headquarters building of the Sagamore Hill Military Reservation c. July 1942. The honorable appellation "first-shirt" was applied to 1st Sgt. Eugene J. Lavoie due to his status of highest-ranking enlisted man in Battery C, handling all administrative matters at post headquarters and acting as an intermediate between officers and enlisted personnel of the unit.

The first newly completed barracks were quickly occupied, but they consisted of very crowded conditions with wood-framed double bunk beds, as pictured. Notice the combat gear—including steel helmets and gas masks—hung from individual bunk ends, footlockers under each bunk, and rifles in circular ready racks.

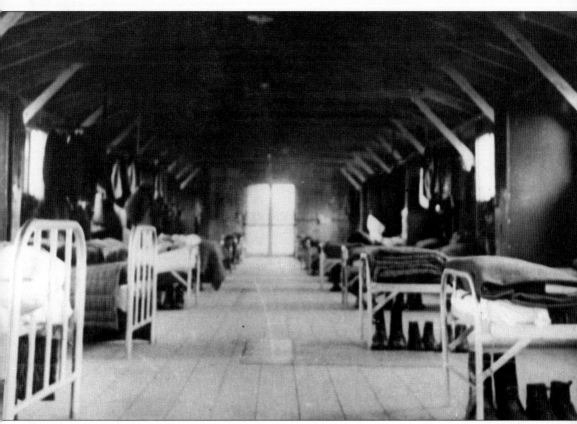

By the end of July 1942, all of the buildings were finalized at Sagamore Hill, and the interiors became more spacious with ample room for each soldier.

The newly constructed mess hall at the Sagamore Hill Military Reservation was spartan in appearance but served excellent food. Notice the Coca Cola machine—at 5¢ per bottle—and wooden bottle racks to the far right.

This is a candid view showing members of the Kitchen Police (KP) doing one of their duties, peeling potatoes outside the mess hall in July 1942.

This was formal beach patrol attire at Sagamore Hill during summer 1942. The unidentified soldier carries all necessary equipment minus the steel helmet—or "pot"—and gas mask.

Looking more like a scene from the Western Desert battle zone, this photograph shows three Battery C soldiers en route to enjoy the refreshment of Cape Cod Bay's salt water and beach.

Beach patrol soldiers from Sagamore Hill have just completed a tiring tour of guard duty during August 1942. Guard duty consisted of 12-hour periods divided into evenly spaced segments patrolling the reservation and resting on portable cots at the administration building.

The Sagamore Hill Military Reservation was a site that many of its young soldiers and some of the sergeants learned to drive the new army jeep. In this view, Sgt. Peter Burke is driving with an unidentified passenger.

Much heavy equipment was necessary to move the cannons, limbers, and other associated material at the Sagamore Hill Military Reservation, including this massive diesel Caterpillar tracked prime hauler.

This is a view of a newly completed Panama Mount, with its 155mm cannon installed at the Sagamore Hill Military Reservation. The design of the Panama Mount allowed for all-around traversing of the cannon upon its central axis, and the low grade of the emplacement afforded sufficient space for recoil during maximum elevation of the weapon when fired. In this image, Private Johnson, one of Battery C's gunners, proudly displays his pet dog perched on top of the gun carriage.

Gun Crew 1 is posing on the 155mm cannon, carriage, and Panama Mount. To the rear is the camouflaged Sagamore Hill battery commander's station.

Gun No. 1—Vicious Virgin—is shown here in its respective gun emplacement, with wooden railroad tie cribwork being constructed by members of the gun crew.

In this view, the rectangular cribwork surrounding Gun No. 2—Big Mary—is nearly completed by personnel at the Sagamore Hill Military Reservation.

This photograph shows Gun No. 1's completed emplacement and one of the gunners with his pet dog.

In this photograph are two North End sergeants in a friendly discussion outside the Sagamore Hill supply room. Sgt. Louis Salza is on the left, and Sgt. Emanuel DiCristoforo, the supply sergeant, is on the right.

Sgt. Emanuel DiCristoforo, supply sergeant of Battery C, is seen here at his desk—also known as his "private domain"—in the Sagamore Hill Military Reservation supply room *c.* 1942.

Members of Battery C are relaxing after the evening meal outside the mess hall at the Sagamore Hill Military Reservation in August 1942.

*Four*

# SAGAMORE HILL:
# FORT SNAFU

This winter 1943 view of the Sagamore Hill Military Reservation shows the main street and buildings covered with snow. The few commercial vehicles parked off the road belong to officers and sergeants.

The camouflage netting for the plotting room in the rear entrance is shown covered with snow and ice following a 1943 snowstorm.

Captain McGill, post and battery commander of Battery C at the Sagamore Hill Military Reservation, is seen in the winter of 1943.

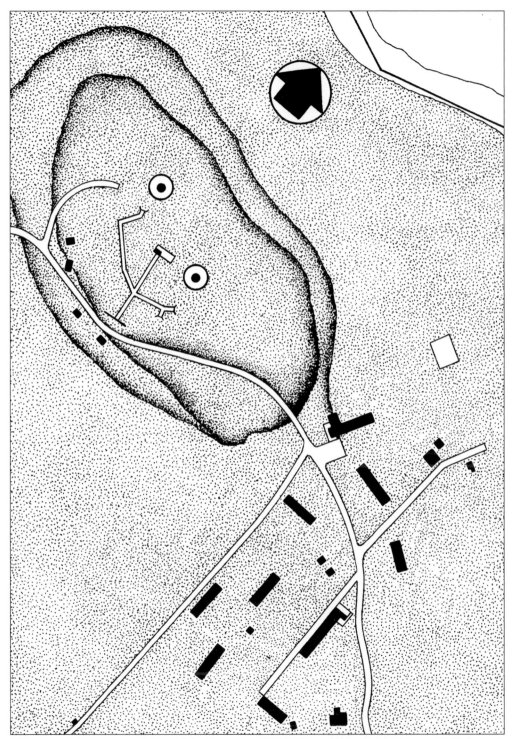

This view shows a general plan of the Sagamore Hill Military Reservation from *c.* 1942 through 1945. The 155mm cannon emplacements are to the upper left, and the barracks, mess hall, administration, supply, and recreation buildings are to the lower right.

From 1943 through 1944, elaborate means of camouflage were established and tested at the Sagamore Hill Military Reservation. Above, a mock roof assembly with netting covers the 155mm cannon exterior. Below is the weapon underlying the camouflage arrangement.

Additional experimental camouflage netting was created at the gun site, including a spring-loaded tripwire unit that would fall away from the gun underneath at a moment's warning. In this view, the soldier on the far right has pulled the net-covered wire to the end of its mechanism stop, where it will be tested again.

In the final version of weaponry camouflage at the Sagamore Hill Military Reservation, the 155mm cannons remained out in the open, surrounded by a layered wall of sandbags, as shown in these photographs.

This photograph shows Gun Crew 1 wearing special designated shirts to be worn for record firing during the summer of 1943.

This is a remarkable photograph of Gun No. 1 at Sagamore Hill being loaded by the gunners prior to record firing in the summer of 1943.

After the cannon was fired for record and the gun crew received their scores, the gun commanders and sergeants were doused in the sponge tub. The large metal tub was filled with water and normally used to slush the gun tube out after firing to extinguish any burning embers of the powder bag after firing. In the image, Pvt. Tony Pisella is being initiated.

This is another image of the dousing ordeal in the 155mm cannon emplacement at Sagamore Hill in July 1943. This rearward view is of Cpl. Lou Salza, gun commander.

The original antiaircraft gun defense in 1942 consisted of two drum-fed, .50-caliber heavy machine guns installed on antiaircraft mounts within a wood-cribbed emplacement.

By 1943, the .50-caliber heavy machine guns had been modified and fitted with new antiaircraft mounts that included sights, armored shields, and counterbalance arrangements.

In addition, the two .50-caliber heavy machine guns were also set up to be used for land defense and antimotor torpedo boat defense. In this view, the weapon is seen firing at a towed target outside the Cape Cod Canal entrance.

The .50-caliber heavy machine gun had a cyclic rate of over 500 rounds per minute and was cooled by a water jacket, which surrounded the barrel. The hose array seen toward the rear of the barrel jacket led to a water-cooling reservoir located on the base of the emplacement.

*Chess*

By the summer of 1943, all new field equipment, including the new style helmet and M-1 Garand rifle, had replaced the post–World War I military issue that Battery C had been issued in 1940. Shown is Sgt. Vincenzo "Chessy" Buscenera.

This is an unidentified infantryman from the 181st Infantry Regiment in class A uniform at Sagamore Hill in 1943. Infantrymen augmented coast artillery personnel of Battery C to guard the roads along the Cape Cod Canal, the Sagamore and Bourne Bridges, and beach patrols.

At varying intervals throughout 1943, additional temporary personnel was assigned to the Sagamore Hill Military Reservation. In this view, technicians from the Harbor Defenses of Boston are posed for a group photograph near the "breakwater barrack."

*Five*

# THE U-BOAT MENACE

The U-boat menace harks back to Sunday, July 21, 1918, when the tugboat *Perth Amboy*, towing four coal barges, was attacked by the German submarine U-156 three miles off Orleans on Cape Cod. The resultant action later became known as the Battle of Orleans and brought unrestricted submarine warfare to the Massachusetts shore. The Battle of Orleans lasted one and a half hours, culminating in the sinking of four barges and severely damaging the *Perth Amboy*, as shown in this grim image. The success of this action activated more submarine attacks off Cape Cod and New England during the early segment of World War II.

As convoys were formed for protection after the 1918 *Perth Amboy* incident, it became commonplace to see swift naval warships navigating the canal, such as the USS *Wadsworth* (Destroyer No. 60), a World War I "four-stacker."

Many allied and neutral nation vessels transited the Cape Cod Canal before America entered the war in 1941. Typical of such pleasure craft is the steel-hulled, three-mast ship believed to be the *7 Seas*, viewed here in the canal in August 1938.

Countless merchant ships from all allied nations plied the Cape Cod Canal prior to World War II. This image shows the *Siamese Prince* of the British Prince Line prior to its being torpedoed and sunk on February 22, 1941.

This is another view of a neutral nation vessel, the tanker *Rio Juramento*, as it transits the Cape Cod Canal *c.* 1940.

Merchant ships were normally unarmed and at the mercy of German submarines, which, rather than expend a valuable torpedo, would surface and sink the target by deck gun. To counter this, a number of merchant ships were equipped with deck guns manned by naval personnel. This image shows the merchant freighter SS *Eskbank* of the Bank Line, fitted with a stern mounted deck gun.

En route to replenish its fuel bunkers, the tanker SS *Melrose* is viewed sailing high and empty in the Cape Cod Canal *c.* 1940.

On January 14, 1942, the Panamanian tanker *Norness* was sunk by U-123, a German submarine, 50 miles south of Martha's Vineyard. In the image, the SS *Explorer*, similar to the *Norness*, is viewed prior to its journey through the Cape Cod Canal.

This photograph shows the Russian icebreaker *Krassin* passing through the Cape Cod Canal on February 14, 1942. The rugged vessel used coal for fuel, as indicated by the tall smokestacks, and bristled with numerous antiaircraft weapons.

At 3:00 a.m. on June 28, 1942, the collier SS *Stephen R. Jones* sheered into the north bank of the Cape Cod Canal, a half mile east of the Bourne Bridge, and began to sink by the bow. When the tide turned later that day, the swift current swung the stricken vessel around toward the south bank and sank, obstructing the waterway. On July 4, 1942, a salvage firm began rapid demolition of the vessel that continued for 28 days and consumed 17.5 tons of dynamite.

When the Cape Cod Canal was closed due to the demolition operations of the SS *Stephen R. Jones* in July 1942, ships and convoys were forced to go around Cape Cod. Six days following the sinking of the SS *Stephen R. Jones*, a freighter was torpedoed and sunk east of the Cape with a loss of 10 crew members. The ship's cargo of various foodstuffs and stock washed up on the Cape's coastline and at the mouth of the Cape Cod Canal, as shown in both images.

This photograph shows additional material washed up on the Cape Cod Canal breakwater. Soldiers from Battery C are inspecting the stock and waterlogged foodstuffs during the little off-duty that was afforded to them.

This is a view of eastbound convoy traffic in the Cape Cod Canal as it generally appeared from 1941 through 1945.

The United Fruit Company operated a number of small banana steamers that sailed between Central America and East Coast ports at the beginning of World War II. In the image, the SS *Abangarez* is viewed in the Cape Cod Canal en route to Boston.

In September 1942, the steamers *Boston* and *New York*—the famous East Coast overnight steamers from New York—departed for duty with the British merchant marine services. Both steamers were fondly remembered as "symbols of the canal." Unfortunately, however, both were sunk by German torpedoes off the Irish coast three weeks after their departure.

This is a view of the British vessel *Myrmidon* passing through the Cape Cod Canal after surviving battle damage on the "Murmansk Run." Convoys that ran between Halifax and Murmansk maintained a low survival ratio due to despicable weather conditions, German submarines, and aircraft attacks. Notice the lifeboats swung out for immediate use, which amplified the dire threat of German submarines off the New England coast in 1942.

This is a somber image of a stricken American tanker being pushed through the Cape Cod Canal by two U.S. Navy vessels c. 1942. The ship has been shelled by deck guns of a German U-boat, causing damage to the superstructure and bridge, numerous burn areas, and loss of power and propulsion.

The British liner *Franconia*—shown above in its peacetime configuration—is steaming through Buzzards Bay en route to the Cape Cod Canal. Below, the liner is shown in its troop ship configuration at the canal *c.* 1942. The *Franconia* was a popular winter transatlantic cruise ship but, in 1939, was pressed into service as a troopship that lasted until 1948. At that time, the Cunard Line refitted the ship for civilian service and sailed from 1949 through 1956. Between 1956 and 1957, the *Franconia* was scrapped in Scotland.

This is a grim November 1943 image of the disabled American oil tanker SS *J.H. Senior* passing under the Bourne vertical lift railroad bridge. The vessel was assisted by four tugboats and shows considerable damage forward of the superstructure. Notice the extended deck platform used to ferry a cargo of fighter aircraft, which have also been wrecked and burned.

In the first seven months of the war, five allied ships had been sunk by German U-boats off Cape Cod. In later months, three additional vessels were sunk, of which one was salvaged. On July 3, 1943, the American freighter SS *Alexander Macomb* was sunk 150 miles east of Cape Cod with a loss of 10 lives. In this 1943 image, a typical Victory ship, en route to be loaded with war supplies, is seen passing through the Cape Cod Canal.

One of the more notable naval accidents occurred at 10:00 p.m. on June 29, 1944, when the USS *Richard W. Suessens* (DE-342) struck the USS *Valor* (Amc-108). The USS *Valor* was a wooden-hulled coastal minesweeper patrolling the southern approach to the Cape Cod Canal near Mishaum Point. The small ship sank in three minutes, and the destroyer and five other ships immediately commenced rescue efforts. Of the 17 men on board that night, 10 were rescued, but the missing 7 were never found. This 1944 image shows a coastal minesweeper of the USS *Valor* type.

The September 14, 1944 hurricane did much damage to the New England coastline, but the most dramatic incident was the loss of the *Vineyard Sound* lightship (LV73, WAL503). The unarmed lightship marked the entrance to Buzzards Bay and Vineyard Sound throughout most of World War II, having been at that station since 1924. Of the 17 crewmen, 12 were lost when the ship sank and 5 were on leave. This facsimile of a 1943 U.S. Coast Guard photograph shows the *Vineyard Sound* armed with a fixed rear deck gun and 20mm antiaircraft guns mounted forward in its limited role as an examination vessel in Buzzards Bay.

On November 16, 1944, the schooner barge *Pottstown*—similar to the *Vale Royal* shown above—was anchored off the Scusset breakwater, near the eastern approach to the Cape Cod Canal, due to heavy fog. A strong northeastern storm set in during the early morning reaching eight on the Beaufort scale, which resulted in the *Pottstown's* hawespipe breaking loose and the anchor chain ripping through the wooden hull to the waterline. The crew from the *Pottstown* was rescued just before it sank. The tugboat *Wathen* of the Red Star Line tried to assist the *Pottstown* and the *Glenside*, another schooner barge, both under the tug's control, but the tug was driven ashore at Town Beach in Sandwich due to a fouled propeller. Coast Guard personnel using a breeches buoy from the Sandwich station rescued its crew, but all three vessels were lost.

Very few large naval ships were able to navigate the Cape Cod Canal during the war. This rare photograph depicts the cruiser USS *San Juan* (CL-54) entering the easterly approach to the canal in 1944.

U.S. Coast Guard ships were on constant patrol in and around the Cape Cod Canal and Buzzards Bay throughout the war, ensuring convoy schedules and making sure shipping proceeded as planned. In this September 1944 image, a Coast Guard patrol boat is weathering hurricane-force winds during a patrol of the canal.

This is a rare and remarkable image of the U.S. Navy light gun cruiser USS *Little Rock* (CL-92),

passing through the Cape Cod Canal in mid-1945.

Naval warships, of all configurations and sizes, constantly steamed through the canal between Boston and Buzzards Bay throughout the war. Shown here is the USS *Bluebird* (AM-72), a minesweeper used to search for magnetic mines sown by German submarines off Boston, Cape Cod Bay, and Newport, Rhode Island sea lanes.

This extraordinary—albeit barely discernible—image depicts the German U-boat U-505, manned by a U.S. Navy crew, passing through the Cape Cod Canal at the war's end. On June 4, 1944, a U.S. Navy task group attacked, boarded, and captured the submarine, but the action was kept secret until 1946, when the craft was scheduled to be a target for naval gun practice. The submarine was saved by the citizens of Chicago, who raised the necessary funds for its installation in the Museum of Science and Industry. In 1954, U-505 was dedicated as a war memorial and remains in place to date.

*Six*

# THE DURATION

Four women are shown sitting on the steps of the recreation building—also called the "Canteen"—at the Sagamore Hill Military Reservation on a Sunday afternoon in August 1944.

In this late-afternoon image, the four women on the steps of the recreation building are accompanied by two of the soldiers from the Sagamore Hill Military Reservation. The photograph below identifies one of the women in the above image as "Miss Sagamore Hill 1944." Both photographs were taken around August 1944.

The Sagamore Hill Military Reservation also served as a nucleus for two additional U.S. Army coast artillery gun sites: one at nearby Sandwich and the other at Rocky Point in Plymouth. The Sandwich installation, initiated in early 1944, was located across the canal from the Sagamore Hill Military Reservation and consisted of a squad of soldiers, a 40mm automatic dual-purpose gun (shown here), and a 60-inch portable searchlight unit. The 40mm antiaircraft gun was emplaced in a sandbagged nest and could be employed against enemy aircraft, antimotor torpedo boats, or land targets.

U.S. Army duty at the Sandwich gun site was not all that dreary, as seen in these group photographs taken in the summer of 1944. Battery C personnel were quartered and fed at the Sandwich Coast Guard Station during their tour of duty at the site.

Off-duty Battery C personnel and two attractive friends are seen here on the Sandwich breakwater during the summer of 1944.

The Rocky Point site, located on the Curtis & Weber Estate, consisted of one or, at varying intervals, two 155mm cannons. The weapons were emplaced in hasty field positions, camouflaged with netting, and manned by personnel from Battery C at the Sagamore Hill Military Reservation. This image shows the arrival of soldiers for their rotating tour of duty at Rocky Point c. 1944.

This is another image depicting members of Battery C prior to their tour of duty at Rocky Point. The soldiers, led by Sgt. Louis Salza (third from the left), remain in the bed of the cargo truck, cheerfully awaiting orders.

Members of the gun crew are shown using a sponge rammer to clean the bore of the 155mm cannon at Rocky Point c. 1944.

Personnel from Battery C at the Rocky Point estate pose near their quarters immediately after an inspection by the battery's commanding officer c. 1944.

This view shows work detail and police call at the Rocky Point installation during the summer of 1944. Police call—according to former Battery C personnel—consisted of "picking up everything that could be, painting anything that couldn't, and saluting everything else!"

Members of Battery C, stationed at Rocky Point, are en route to formal military proceedings in Plymouth c. 1944. Sgt. Louis Salza, in charge of the group, is in the back row to the far left.

"Sergeants III" at the Rocky Point site are seen posing outside their quarters on the estate during the summer of 1944.

In 1944, the Coast Guard personnel at the Sandwich station gave the soldiers at Sagamore Hill an old lifeboat to use during the summer months. The soldiers spent many off-duty hours rowing outside the canal—as viewed in the above image—and inspecting the wreck *Vale Royal*. In the photograph below, the soldiers and their small boat are shown directly under the bow of the *Vale Royal*.

When the soldiers boarded the *Vale Royal*, the acute angle of the wreck made standing erect and keeping balance quite a task, as viewed in this photograph.

Two members of the Sagamore Hill Military Reservation defy gravity by standing upright on the starboard side of the *Vale Royal c.* 1944.

USO entertainers frequented the Sagamore Hill Military Reservation throughout the war, as evidenced by the two images of a troupe visiting the site in August 1944. This particular USO show consisted of complex lariat tricks and demonstrations by the three civilian entertainers shown in the photograph below.

Battery C personnel are seen outside the rear door of the recreation room—also referred to as the "Stage Door Canteen"—at the Sagamore Hill Military Reservation.

This photograph shows the supply sergeant, Emanuel DiCristoforo, with his assistant, Pasquale DellaPiana, and the supply room's pet dog. Sergeant DiCristoforo trained the dog to growl at anyone entering the supply room requesting supplies.

The Battery C orderly room detail is shown outside the Sagamore Hill Military Reservation administration building or post headquarters c. 1944.

The most popular vehicle at the Sagamore Hill Military Reservation was the ubiquitous one-quarter-ton jeep. The vehicle shown was assigned to the battery commander and driven—for the most part—by the orderly room clerk, "Guy" Bailey. Both images were taken in 1944.

This is a view of the Sagamore Hill Military Reservation's motor pool in the summer of 1944. The image above depicts two mechanics in the front of the building, and the photograph below captures two drivers resting on the fender of a tactical troop truck.

This is another summer 1944 view of the Sagamore Hill Military Reservation motor pool following an ordnance and quartermaster corps inspection by officers and technicians from the headquarters of the Harbor Defenses of Boston. Vehicles shown, beginning on the far left, are command cars, light cargo trucks, and large two-and-a-half-ton cargo trucks, one being equipped with a snow plow attachment.

A relaxing moment follows a strenuous formal inspection of personnel and tactical motor vehicles at the Sagamore Hill Military Reservation. In addition to a jeep and command car, the site was also authorized a number of cargo and troop trucks, one of which is shown here.

This view of the Sagamore Hill Military Reservation mess hall entrance shows the mess sergeant, with cleaver, and his assistant, with potato masher, c. 1944.

This photograph is of the "Sagamore Smiling Sentinel," Pfc. William Maynard, who was probably one of the very few sentinels who laughed before a tour of duty at the Sagamore Hill Military Reservation during World War II.

*Seven*

# OTHER CANAL DEFENSES

While the Sagamore Hill Military Reservation protected the eastern approach to the Cape Cod Canal, other modern coastal defense systems ranging from massive cannons to rapid-fire gun batteries were employed to defend the canal. The crowded conditions in New York necessitated naval authorities to move the convoy assembly area bound for the United Kingdom to Buzzards Bay. This area, known as the western approach to the canal, fell under the jurisdiction of the Harbor Defenses of New Bedford, headquartered at Fort Rodman, shown in this 1944 aerial view.

This image depicts an identical weapon system to Battery Milliken, the massive long-range, 12-inch gun emplacement at Fort Rodman in its underground, reinforced-concrete casemate.

This interior view of a 12-inch gun emplacement gun room shows the weapon, carriage, and shell-ramming apparatus. Camouflage netting has been stretched over the front of the reinforced-concrete casemate.

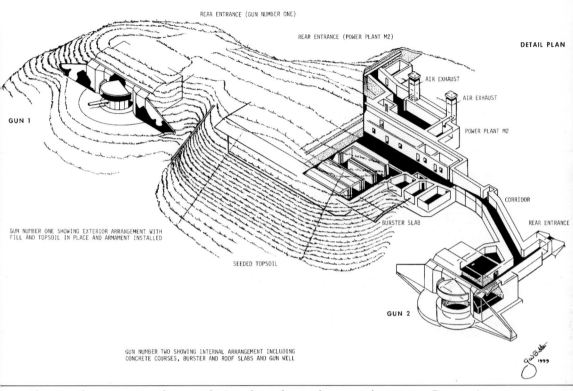

REAR ENTRANCE (GUN NUMBER ONE)

REAR ENTRANCE (POWER PLANT M2)

AIR EXHAUST

AIR EXHAUST

POWER PLANT M2

GUN 1

CORRIDOR

REAR ENTRANCE

GUN NUMBER ONE SHOWING EXTERIOR ARRANGEMENT WITH
FILL AND TOPSOIL IN PLACE AND ARMAMENT INSTALLED

BURSTER SLAB

SEEDED TOPSOIL

GUN 2

GUN NUMBER TWO SHOWING INTERNAL ARRANGEMENT INCLUDING
CONCRETE COURSES, BURSTER AND ROOF SLABS AND GUN WELL

This is a phantom view of a typical 12-inch modernized gun emplacement—Battery Augustus P. Gardner, located at Fort Ruckman in Nahant, Massachusetts.

The Mishaum Point Military Reservation in South Dartmouth, Massachusetts, is shown c. 1945. The image to the left depicts the Harbor Entrance Control Post (HECP) that controlled all military activity within Buzzards Bay and the western approach to the Cape Cod Canal during World War II. The blister atop the roof contained an SCR-682 short-range radar unit. Within months of deactivation, the station had been vandalized, as shown below.

This is a 200-series gun emplacement typical of the style situated at Mishaum Point. A heavy, cast-steel shield contains the six-inch gun, and the ammunition, power, and plotting areas are protected by a thick, reinforced-concrete casemate, or "bunker," seen to the right.

A 200-series gun at Fort Dearborn, New Hampshire, is being readied to fire. Nearly identical in operation and appearance, the six-inch guns fired a 95-pound shell, maintained a range of 15 miles, and were capable of all-around fire.

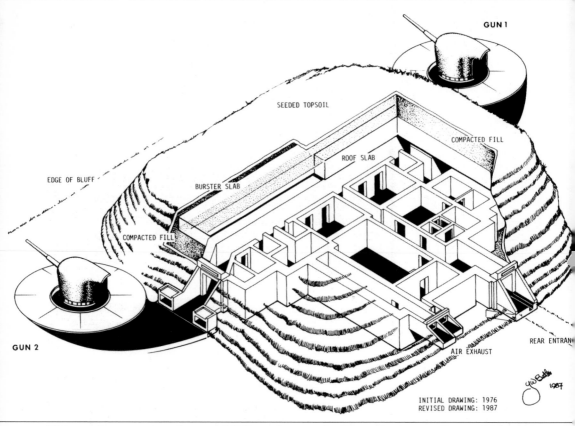

GUN 1

SEEDED TOPSOIL

COMPACTED FILL

ROOF SLAB

EDGE OF BLUFF

BURSTER SLAB

COMPACTED FILL

GUN 2

REAR ENTRAN

AIR EXHAUST

INITIAL DRAWING: 1976
REVISED DRAWING: 1987

This is a phantom view of a typical 200-series, six-inch gun emplacement—Battery 206 at East Point in Nahant, Massachusetts.

This is a view of the plotting room of Battery 210 at Mishaum Point. The sergeant is pointing to the plotting board layout, which represents the gun battery range of fire. Notice the Elizabeth Island chain and point of origin of the gun battery at South Dartmouth.

This view shows the power room of Battery 210 at Mishaum Point. The sergeant is standing next to the distribution panel, which controls commercial, base, and gun emplacement power systems. The three diesel-electric generators are 125kva and silenced by huge mufflers in an adjacent chamber.

This partial view of Battery 210 in 1946 shows the gun tube removed and prepared for reissue or salvage. Located to the rear of the shield is the HECP and, to the left, is an SCR-296 long-range radar assembly mounted atop the steel-girder tower.

This is a front view of a 200-series six-inch gun and shield with the author adjacent. The photograph was taken at Fort Pickens, Florida, in July 1982.

To complement the two 155mm cannons at the Sagamore Hill Military Reservation, two additional cannon batteries were situated at the western approach to the Cape Cod Canal. Both batteries consisted of two cannons each, installed on Panama Mounts, and were located at Butler's Point and Mishaum Point, respectively.

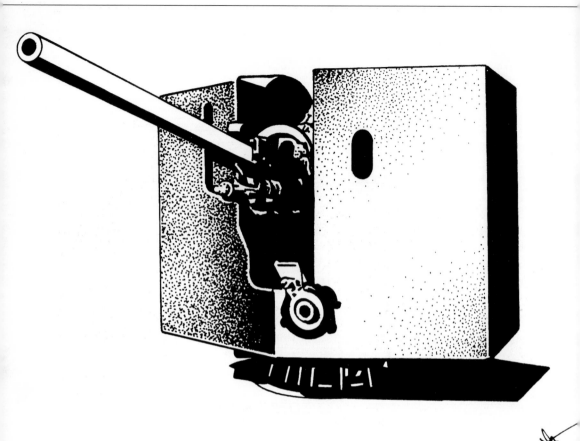

This illustration depicts a shielded 90mm gun in its antimotor torpedo boat role. Batteries of this rapid-fire gun were placed at strategic locations throughout Buzzards Bay to thwart any attempt by enemy motor torpedo boats or surfaced submarine attacks. The batteries of fixed 90mm guns, mounted in pairs, were located at AMTB Battery 931, Barney's Joy Point; AMTB Battery 932, Cuttyhunk Island; AMTB Battery 933, Nashawena Island; and AMTB Battery 934, Butler's Point. In most instances, each battery of two fixed-gun mounts was supplemented by two 90mm guns on carriages, placed nearby.

Shown are two images of a 90mm AMTB battery. The view above depicts a 90mm gun being loaded by the gun crew, and the photograph below shows a 90mm gun with its supportive .50-caliber heavy machine gun in its sandbagged nest. Both photographs were taken on Great Brewster Island in Boston Harbor *c.* 1943.

By 1943, target acquisition and tracking was through electronic means consisting of a radical new device termed "radar," capable of supplying continuous data in darkness, fog, and for many miles in distance. To support the 12-inch and 6-inch gun batteries in Buzzards Bay, two installations of SCR-296-A radar sets were mounted atop high steel-girder towers, which are shown in this image.

Target tracking was mostly accomplished by visual means through 1943, when radar was introduced to harbor defenses. Concrete observation towers—similar to the rectangular manhole type shown here—were situated at strategic locations and contained powerful telescopes, or range finders, to visually provide fire-control data to their respective gun battery.

This is a view of a standard fire control tower used for target tracking and observation. A reinforced-concrete hood protected each observation level over the viewing aperture, protecting the observers from shrapnel and debris if necessary. The tower shown—located at the Harris Estate in Nahant, Massachusetts—was of the six-level type with three separate observing rooms.

Target illumination of surface and aerial targets were provided by powerful 60-inch diameter searchlights located at prominent seafront areas. This image depicts a General Electric 60-inch searchlight mounted on a steel-girder tower assembly.

The most common version of the searchlight was the trailer-mounted unit shown in this image. This General Electric 60-inch searchlight could be used for surface surveillance or tracking and for antiaircraft purposes. Sophisticated remote-control devices and early radar arrays (SCR-268) also brought searchlights into use during night antiaircraft drills. The cables in the foreground led to mobile power supply and data-transmission devices as required by the searchlight assignment.

*Eight*

# CLOSURE

The Sagamore Hill Military Reservation was terminated on April 1, 1945. On November 5, 1945, the U.S. Coast Guard and U.S. Navy relinquished control of the Cape Cod Canal to the U.S. Army Corps of Engineers. This image shows the overall condition of the site today.

This is a 2002 image depicting the center of the main cantonment of the Sagamore Hill Military Reservation. The gun battery was situated beyond the left-hand road and is now obscured by tree and brush growth.

The photograph above shows Gun No. 1 of the Sagamore Hill Military Reservation in 1942. The image below shows the identical area in 2002 after volunteers from AmeriCorps—under the U.S. Army Corps of Engineers parks personnel supervision—cleared brush and debris from the gun mount proper.

Above is the Panama Mount of Gun No. 2 of the Sagamore Hill Military Reservation in 2002, and below are two ammunition storage units, or "igloos," situated to the rear of each gun mount proper.

This is a view of the ammunition storage igloos of Gun No. 1 at Sagamore Hill. The corrugated-steel shelters were assembled by members of the gun crew (resulting in many bruised knuckles and infamous army oaths) and were covered with sandbags when completed for both protection and camouflage.

Pictured is a restored Panama Mount emplacement—identical to the two units at the Sagamore Hill Military Reservation—on the eastern seaboard. Most of the concrete emplacements existing at present have been either filled or covered with ground cover. This exemplary unit is located at the tip of Fort Dearborn Park in Rye, New Hampshire.

This image shows a fine overall example of a 155mm cannon on a Panama Mount at the Salisbury Beach Military Reservation c. 1944. A fire hose is in use by the gun crew to wet down the surrounding sand area prior to the gun firing. Notice to the rear of the emplacement a number of wooden wedges that cover the open segments of the recoil pit when the gun is not active.

Above is a present-day view of the Sagamore breakwater of the Cape Cod Canal. It is in this area that a .50-caliber heavy machine gun nest—shown below—was established during World War II.

# ACKNOWLEDGMENTS

Most photographs in this work were provided through the kindness of Louis Salza in Lexington, Massachusetts. Without his images and vast knowledge of the Sagamore Hill Military Reservation, this pictorial history would not be possible. Sergeant Salza was stationed at the Sagamore Hill Military Reservation from its concept in December 1941 through its termination in early 1945.

Special appreciation is due to the personnel of the U.S. Army Corps of Engineers, New England District, Cape Cod Canal Field Office, who were extremely courteous and helpful regarding access to army records and the photographic archives of the Cape Cod Canal. William F. Norman—park manager and friend longstanding—allowed departmental time to access records and ensure the accuracy of data presented in this pictorial history. Credit is due to Samantha Mirabella and Roger F. Hagen, park rangers, who spent a goodly amount of time researching various factors and dates, and John Pribilla, park ranger, who devoted considerable time sharing his voluminous wealth of knowledge and a detailed tour of the former Sagamore Hill Military Reservation.

Other images were provided by the Associated Press (via Christopher MacDonald); the U.S. Army History Institute; the Marine Science Center, New Hampshire; the New Bedford Standard Times; the Walker Transportation Collection of the Beverly Historical Society, Beverly, Massachusetts; Col. Gilroy F. Linehan Jr.; and Christopher MacDonald, New Bedford.

All illustrations are by the author, Gerald Butler, Seacoast Fortification Historian.

Sgt. Louis Salza relaxes with his pet dog at the Sagamore Hill Military Reservation with his pet dog in 1944.